Test Preparation

Writing Essentials, Mathematics Review, & Reasoning Skills

Dr. Cassundra White-Elliott

CLF Publishing, LLC.
9161 Sierra Ave, Ste. 203C
Fontana, CA 92335
www.clfpublishing.org

Copyright © 2017 by Cassundra White-Elliott. All rights reserved. No portion of this book may be reproduced, stored in a retrieval system, or transmitted by any form or any means electronically, photocopied, recorded, or any other except for brief quotations in printed reviews, without the prior permission of the publisher.

Cover design by *Senir Design*. Contact information- info@senirdesign.com.

ISBN # 978-1-945102-23-3

Printed in the United States of America.

Table of Contents

Reading Comprehension/Written Expression Workbook   5

Grammar and Punctuation Diagnostic Test   7

Reading and Vocabulary   9

Vocabulary Worksheet   17

Sentence Structure   21

Spelling Worksheets   25

Reading Comprehension Practice   29

Final Grammar Test   33

Mathematics Review Workbook   41

Math Prescreening Assessment   43

Algebra Diagnostic Test   51

Percent and Ratio Practice Test   59

Percentage Word Problems   63

Mean, Median, Mode   65

Distance, Rate, Time   68

Mathematics Review Guide   71

Data Interpretation & Reasoning Workbook   79

Analytical Reasoning Test 81

Data Interpretation Practice 83

Numerical Reasoning Practice 89

READING COMPREHENSION/ WRITTEN EXPRESSION WORKBOOK

Grammar and Punctuation—Diagnostic Test

Read the following sentences and correct any errors in the space provided below.

1. Tossing and turning in bed, the clock struck midnight.

2. The weather reporter predicted snow and that it only last the morning.

3. In it's recent report, the finance committee were critical of the initial stock option.

4. The magazine staff are composed almost entirely of newly graduated college students.

5. Gazing upon the mystical cards, the cynical man's future was predicted by the tarot reader.

6. Anyone can learn how to juggle if they want to.

7. The team discussed what needed to be improved, the team wanted to win the state championship.

8. His wife asked him to be quiet she was reading and didn't want to be disturbed.

9. The management classes are interesting, enjoyable, and to the student's advantage.

10. Dave uploaded the new software to the network server and, he submitted all the warranty paperwork.

11. Although Carel had never visited Paducah, Kentucky he knew on which river it was located.

12. Susan camped at the base of the mountain, however, she did not hike to the peak.

13. Because the misprint in the newspaper showed the computers on sale for only a dollar; the manufacturer lost a lot of money.

14. Either Mr. Jacobs or Ms. Hill forgot to set their cell phone to vibrate.

15. Did you say that Jared and him will be promoted?

16. A hockey team is relatively small. They don't have as many players as a football team.

17. Managers in several offices around the globe has to be consulted.

18. Our financial department did not approve of him investing in highly speculative deals.

19. The apartment we saw yesterday was the best of the two.

20. Due to the fact that dogs are color blind, Joe ceased and desisted in teaching his dog to fetch the blue slippers.

21. Our costs for outsourcing our customer service are exorbitant, and may become higher if we don't limit the use of direct mailings.

22. The hiring committee puts little weight on grade point averages, hence, focus the resume on your work experience.

23. The school, that has the best resources, will attract the most students.

24. "The city cannot afford", the mayor said "to supplement the cost of Internet access".

25. After the crew members arrived, they should of started signing the log books.

Reading and Vocabulary

Jane Austen. *Pride and Prejudice,* **From Chapter 3**

Mr. Bingley was good-looking and gentlemanlike; he had a pleasant countenance, and easy, unaffected manners. His sisters were fine women, with an air of decided fashion. His brother-in-law, Mr. Hurst, merely looked the gentleman; but his friend Mr. Darcy soon drew the attention of the room by his fine, tall person, handsome features, noble mien, and the report which was in general circulation within five minutes after his entrance, of his having ten thousand a year. The gentlemen pronounced him to be a fine figure of a man, the ladies declared he was much handsomer than Mr. Bingley, and he was looked at with great admiration for about half the evening, till his manners gave a disgust which turned the tide of his popularity; for he was discovered to be proud; to be above his company, and above being pleased; and not all his large estate in Derbyshire could then save him from having a most forbidding, disagreeable countenance, and being unworthy to be compared with his friend.

Mr. Bingley had soon made himself acquainted with all the principal people in the room; he was lively and unreserved, danced every dance, was angry that the ball closed so early, and talked of giving one himself at Netherfield. Such amiable qualities must speak for themselves. What a contrast between him and his friend! Mr. Darcy danced only once with Mrs. Hurst and once with Miss Bingley, declined being introduced to any other lady, and spent the rest of the evening in walking about the room, speaking occasionally to one of his own party. His character was decided. He was the proudest, most disagreeable man in the world, and everybody hoped that he would never come there again. Amongst the most violent against him was Mrs. Bennet, whose dislike of his general [behavior] was sharpened into particular resentment by his having slighted one of her daughters.

Define Each Word

- countenance _____
- unaffected _____

- mien _____
- forbidding _____
- slighted _____

Write the Correct Word from the Vocabulary

1. Mrs. Jones's (m)_____ was very regal, so she gave the impression of being aloof and standoffish, but she was actually very friendly.

2. The rocks along the coast presented a _____ obstacle to the scouts, but the scoutmaster's instructions and encouragement allowed them to reach the lighthouse.

3. Because of the stern and imposing aspect of Jack's (c)_____ , he did not make many friends at work.

4. Vivian felt _____ because Angela did not invite her to the party.

5. The friendly smile from the server appeared _____ and genuine, not merely a ploy to earn a large gratuity.

Nathaniel Hawthorne. From "Young Goodman Brown"

Young Goodman Brown came forth at sunset into the street at Salem village; but put his head back, after crossing the threshold, to exchange a parting kiss with his young wife. And Faith, as the wife was aptly named, thrust her own pretty head into the street, letting the wind play with the pink ribbons of her cap while she called to Goodman Brown.

"Dearest heart," whispered she, softly and rather sadly, when her lips were close to his ear, "prithee put off your journey until sunrise and sleep in your own bed to-night. A lone woman is troubled with such dreams and such thoughts that she's afeard of herself sometimes. Pray tarry with me this night, dear husband, of all nights in the year."

"My love and my Faith," replied young Goodman Brown, "of all nights in the year, this one night must I tarry away from thee. My journey, as thou callest it, forth and back again, must needs be done 'twixt now and sunrise. What, my sweet, pretty wife, dost thou doubt me already, and we but three months married?"

"Then God bless you!" said Faith, with the pink ribbons; "and may you find all well when you come back."

"Amen!" cried Goodman Brown. "Say thy prayers, dear Faith, and go to bed at dusk, and no harm will come to thee."

So they parted; and the young man pursued his way until, being about to turn the corner by the meeting-house, he looked back and saw the head of Faith still peeping after him with a melancholy air, in spite of her pink ribbons.

"Poor little Faith!" thought he, for his heart smote him. "What a wretch am I to leave her on such an errand! She talks of dreams, too. Methought as she spoke there was trouble in her face, as if a dream had warned her what work is to be done tonight. But no, no; 't would kill her to think it. Well, she's a blessed angel on earth; and after this one night I'll cling to her skirts and follow her to heaven."

Define Each Word

- aptly
- dusk
- peep
- melancholy
- smite

Write the Correct Word from the Vocabulary

1. The toddler _____ shyly through the window as the mail carrier delivered the large package.

2. As it often happens during war time, the soldier was _____ with the love for the beautiful young widow.

3. Joe's daughter, Hope, was _____ named because she was an eternal optimist, always believing the best.

4. When Pruna's grandmother died, a _____ air filled her house for many years.

5. The mosquitoes emerged from the mangroves around Chapman Field Park at _____, just after sunset.

W. E. B. Du Bois. The Souls of Black Folk -- From Chapter 1, "On the Dawn of Freedom"

In the work of establishing the Negroes as peasant proprietors, the [Freedmen's] Bureau was from the first handicapped and at last absolutely checked. Something was done, and larger things were planned; abandoned lands were leased so long as they remained in the hands of the Bureau, and a total revenue of nearly half a million dollars derived from black tenants. Some other lands to which the nation had gained title were sold on easy terms, and public lands were opened for settlement to the very few freedmen who had tools and capital. But the vision of "forty acres and a mule" -- the righteous and reasonable ambition to become a landholder, which the nation had all but categorically promised the freedmen -- was destined in most cases to bitter disappointment. And those men of marvelous hindsight who are today seeking to preach the Negro back to the present peonage of the soil know well, or ought to know, that the opportunity of binding the Negro peasant willingly to the soil was lost on that day when the Commissioner of the Freedmen's Bureau had to go to South Carolina and tell the weeping freedmen, after their years of toil, that their land was not theirs, that there was a mistake -- somewhere. If by 1874 the Georgia Negro alone owned three hundred and fifty thousand acres of land, it was by grace of his thrift rather than by bounty of the government.

The greatest success of the Freedmen's Bureau lay in the planting of the free school among Negroes, and the idea of free elementary education among all classes in the South. It not only called the school-mistresses through the benevolent agencies and built them schoolhouses, but it helped discover and support such apostles of human culture as Edmund Ware, Samuel Armstrong, and Erastus Cravath. The opposition to Negro education in the South was at first bitter, and showed itself in ashes, insult, and blood; for the South believed an educated Negro to be a dangerous Negro. And the South was not wholly wrong; for education among all kinds of men always has had, and always will have, an element of danger and revolution, of dissatisfaction and discontent. Nevertheless, men strive to know. Perhaps some inkling of this paradox, even in the unquiet days of the Bureau, helped the bayonets allay an opposition to human training which still to-day lies smoldering in the South, but not flaming. Fisk, Atlanta, Howard, and Hampton were founded in these days, and six million dollars were expended for educational work, seven hundred and fifty thousand dollars of which the freedmen themselves gave of their poverty.

Define Each Word

- proprietor
- tenant
- benevolent
- paradox
- allay

Write the Correct Word from the Vocabulary

1. Some citizens viewed the despot as a _____ dictator because his regime provided free medical care and primary education.

2. In order to _____ any suspicion that the cheating scandal involving the athletes was condoned, the administration expelled seven players and an assistant coach.

3. After her partner's death, Camile became the sole _____ of the beauty salon.

4. That extreme poverty and sublime riches exist side by side seems like a _____ to many.

5. If the recently unemployed _____ does not pay rent, he will be evicted.

Aesop. Fables. "The Fox and the Goat"

A Fox, having fallen into a well, could find no means of escape. A Goat, overcome with thirst, came to the well, and, seeing the Fox, inquired if the water was good. The Fox, concealing his sad plight under a merry guise, indulged in lavish praise of the water, saying it was beyond measure excellent, and encouraged him to descend. The Goat, mindful only of his thirst, thoughtlessly jumped down, when, just as he quenched his thirst, the Fox informed him of the difficulty they were both in, and suggested a scheme for their common escape. "If," said he, "you will place your fore-feet upon the wall, and bend your head, I will run up your back and escape, and will help you out." On the Goat readily assenting to this proposal, the Fox leaped upon his back, and steadying himself with the goat's horns reached in safety the mouth of the well, and immediately made off as fast as he could. The Goat upbraided him with the breach of his bargain, when he turned round and cried out: "You foolish fellow! If you had as many brains in your head as you have hairs in your beard, you would never have gone down before you had inspected the way up, nor have exposed yourself to dangers from which you had determined upon no means of escape."

Look before you leap.

Define Each Word
- plight
- guise
- indulge
- assent
- breach

Write the Correct Word from the Vocabulary

1. Despite his doctor's advice, the ravenous gourmand _____ in large portions of richly decadent chocolate, butter-cream cake.

2. It took two weeks for the poorly-armed rebels to _____ the royal army's main fortifications and to capture the ousted king.

3. Mother Teresa was unusually sensitive to the _____ of the poor and the disenfranchised.

4. The arms dealer merely nodded in _____ when he agreed to the price for six million AK-47 assault rifles to be sold to the war lord.

5. Under the _____ of filial devotion, the unscrupulous daughter secured a large inheritance by flattering her ailing father constantly during the last year of his life.

Vocabulary Worksheet

1. What is the missing letter in the following word: VERT_BRATE?

a. A

b. E

c. I

d. O

2. What is the spelling of the word that means "of the night"?

a. Nocturnal

b. Noucturnal

c. Nocturnel

d. Nochturnal

3. What is the meaning of the prefix "dia"?

a. Double

b. Across

c. Opposite

d. Negation

4. What is the spelling of the word that means "laying on paint thickly"?

a. Imposto

b. Empasto

c. Impostto

d. Impasto

5. What is the spelling of the word that means "a precious stone of a sky-blue color"?

a. Tirquoise

b. Turquise

c. Turquoise

d. Turquoi

6. The correct spelling of a word meaning "a cutting instrument" is which of the following?

a. Sciscor

b. Scissor

c. Sissor

d. Sizzor

7. What does the prefix "hemi" mean?

a. Half

b. Incomplete

c. Part

d. Section

8. What is the missing letter in the following word: GREN_DIER?

a. A

b. I

c. E

d. O

9. The correct spelling of a word meaning "to store underground" is which of the following?

a. Cach

b. Cashe

c. Cash

d. Cache

10. What is the meaning of the suffix "ary"?

a. Of the air

b. Of the essence of

c. Connected with

d. Enlightening

11. What is the missing letter in the following word: _ OCUNDITY?

a. T

b. S

c. D

d. J

12. What is the meaning of the word that means "having qualities of a statute"?

a. Statuesche

b. Statuesque

c. Statutesque

d. Statusque

13. What does the prefix "peri" mean?

a. Around
b. Boundary
c. To walk
d. View

14. What is the missing letter in the following word: ELECTROL_TE?

a. I
b. IE
c. Y
d. U

15. What does the suffix "escent" mean?

a. Bubbly
b. Essence
c. Becoming
d. Rising

16. What is the missing letter in the following word: _DOMETER?

a. I
b. E
c. A
d. U

Sentence Structure

A **sentence** is a set of words that is complete in itself, typically containing a subject and predicate, conveying a statement, question, exclamation, or command, and consisting of a main clause and sometimes one or more subordinate clauses.

A **sentence fragment** is a group of words that is only part of a **sentence** and does not express a complete thought. Usually **sentence fragments** are pieces of **sentences** that have become disconnected from the main clauses. In addition, a **sentence** without a subject or without a predicate is a **fragment** of a complete **sentence**.

A comma splice is the incorrect use of a comma instead of a conjunction to link two independent clauses.

A **run-on** is a **sentence** in which two or more independent clauses (i.e., complete sentences) are joined without an appropriate punctuation or conjunction. Although this is generally considered a stylistic error, it is occasionally used in literature and may be used as a rhetorical device.

Sentence Fragments Exercise 1

DIRECTIONS: Determine which of the following word groups are sentence fragments and which are complete sentences. ■ If the group of words is a complete sentence, write S. ■ If the group of words is a fragment, write F.

_____ 1. If your parents think today's fashions are weird.

_____ 2. They should see the clothes people wore in the Middle Ages.

_____ 3. Patterns of floral or geometric shapes popular.

_____ 4. Liked clothes that were half one color and half another.

_____ 5. Might have one green leg and one red leg.

_____ 6. People often heavy leather belts decorated with metal and jewels.

_____ 7. Edges of clothing into shapes called dagges.

_____ 8. Sleeves with streamers that were two or three feet long.

_____ 9. Shoes had long toes that were padded to retain their shape.

_____10. Tights of velvet or silk.

_____11. When clothes were edged and lined in fur.

_____12. Layers very common in medieval clothing.

_____13. Was a way of displaying wealth.

_____14. The more clothes a person could afford to wear, the wealthier that person was.

_____15. Might wear a short-sleeved tunic over a long-sleeved tunic, with a sleeveless mantle over all.

_____16. The usual head covering for men a hood with an attached shoulder cape and a long, extended point, like a tail.

_____17. Women wore a neckcloth pinned to their braids, hiding their hair.

_____18. On top of the head, would wear a veil, a linen crown, or a small, round hat.

_____19. In the later Middle Ages, women wore jeweled metal nets over their coiled braids.

_____20. Current fashions a little boring in comparison.

Sentence Fragments Exercise 2

DIRECTIONS Determine which of the following word groups are sentence fragments and which are complete sentences. ■ If the group of words is a complete sentence, write S. ■ If the group of words is a fragment, write F.

_____ 1. Antarctica has the highest average elevation of the seven continents.

_____ 2. No native people on Antarctica.

_____ 3. Because it is too cold.

_____ 4. Although scientists and other workers live in Antarctica for about a year at a time.

_____ 5. These people there to study many things.

_____ 6. Examine the ozone layer, sleep patterns, and fish survival in subzero temperatures.

_____ 7. Ninety-five percent of Antarctica covered with ice.

_____ 8. Antarctica approximately 70 percent of the world's fresh water in its ice.

_____ 9. Even though Antarctica is covered in ice and snow, it can be considered a desert.

_____ 10. A desert an area that gets very little precipitation.

_____ 11. Antarctica receives only two inches of rain each year.

_____ 12. Also has very high winds.

_____ 13. Sometimes winds as high as 200 miles per hour.

_____ 14. Many animals in the ocean around Antarctica.

_____ 15. Include whales and seals.

_____ 16. One type of bird found on Antarctica is the penguin.

_____ 17. Antarctica so isolated that its snow and ice are very pure.

_____ 18. The continent is far away from pollution.

_____ 19. A mountain range across the continent.

_____ 20. Antarctica's Mount Erebus an active volcano.

Sentence Structure Exercise 3

DIRECTIONS Decide which of the following groups of words are run-on sentences. ■ If the group of words is correct, write C; if it is a run-on, write R.

_____ 1. Brown bears include the grizzly and the kodiak, the largest brown bear is the kodiak.

_____ 2. Kodiak bears weigh as much as 1,700 pounds, they grow to a height of ten feet.

_____ 3. Bears can live more than 30 years in the wild.

_____ 4. Bears' sense of smell is more developed than their hearing or sight.

_____ 5. Females give birth to as many as four cubs, the cubs stay with their mother two

or three years.

_____ 6. Many people are afraid of bears, encounters with bears are actually infrequent.

_____ 7. Grizzly bears are solitary animals, they do not want to interact with people.

_____ 8. Generally, bears attack only when they are surprised, or when they are protecting

their young.

_____ 9. People should always store food and garbage properly, bears could be attracted by

the smell.

_____ 10. Never try to outrun a bear, it can run more than 30 miles per hour.

Spelling Worksheet #1

Q1 - Which is the correct spelling?

☐ Accomodation

☐ Accommodation

Q2 - Which is the correct spelling?

☐ Necesary

☐ Necessary

Q3 - Which is the correct spelling?

☐ Difficulty

☐ Dificulty

Q4 - Which is the correct spelling?

☐ Prettier

☐ Prettyer

Q5 - Which is the correct spelling?

☐ Writting

☐ Writing

Q6 - Which is the correct spelling?

☐ Which

☐ Wich

Q7 - Which is the correct spelling?

☐ Tried

☐ Tryed

Q8 - Which is the correct spelling?

☐ Plaied

☐ Played

Q9 - Which is the correct spelling?

☐ Biger

☐ Bigger

Q10 - Which is the correct spelling?

☐ Welcomming

☐ Welcoming

Q11 - Which is the correct spelling?

☐ Embarrasment

☐ Embarrassment

Q12 - Which is the correct spelling?

☐ Priveleged

☐ Privileged

Q13 - Which is the correct spelling?

☐ Panel

☐ Pannel

Q14 - Which is the correct spelling?

☐ Professional

☐ Proffessional

Q15 - Which is the correct spelling?

☐ Adress

☐ Addres

☐ Address

Spelling Worksheet #2

Spelling and Usage

Choose the correct word(s) to complete the sentences below.

1. We had fewer/less items than the allowed limit, so we were able to use the express line where there are fewer/less people waiting.

2. I thought about stealing the money, but I knew my conscious/conscience would bother me if I did; even if I was never caught, I would always be conscious/conscience of my theft.

3. There/they're/their were so many things I wanted to say to him, but since his friends were there/ they're/their, I said nothing and just waited for there/they're/their departure.

4. Its/It's true that some readers have scene/seen the poem as pedantic, but I thought the work and its/it's message were important and interesting.

5. The very site/cite/sight of the book is enough to bring tears to my eyes; its/it's cover and language are so beautiful that in every paper I write, I feel compelled to cite/sight/site an excerpt from it.

6. Whomever/whoever wins the lottery will be a multimillionaire; I hope he or she will remember all those who/whom have been good to them.

7. My older sister is taller than I/me. Please RSVP to the party by sending an e-mail to Silas or I/me.

8. I finally gained access/excess/assess/except to the website with my log-in information, but once I logged in, I could not access/excess/assess/except how well I was doing with the assigned work.

9. How much farther/further will we have to drive in this car? I could not read his hand-drawn map, so I asked him to explain it to me farther/further.

10. I feel good/well today; I think I did very good/well on my test.

Reading Comprehension Practice

Read the following passages and answer the corresponding questions, demonstrating your understanding of the information, in each passage.

Passage #1
Research suggests that there are creatures that do not know what light means at the bottom of **the** sea. They don't have either eyes or ears; they can only feel. There is no day or night for them. There are no winters, no summers, no sun, no moon, and no **stars.** It is **as** if a child spent its life in darkness in bed, **with** nothing to see or hear. How different our own life is! Sight shows us the ground beneath our feet and the heavens above us - the sun, moon, and stars, shooting stars, lightning, and the sunset. It shows us day and night. We are able to hear voices, the sound of the sea, and music. We feel, we taste, we smell. How fortunate we are!

Reading Comprehension Questions

1. Judging from the passage, we *can* **say that this story is** mainly about ..... .
a) life of sea creatures at the bottom of the sea
b) how changes in the seasons are perceived by the deep-sea creatures
c) how wonderful our lives were and will be
d) the differences among creatures of the **earth** and those of the sea
e) the superiority of human beings over some creatures in terms of senses

2. We discover that the sea creatures in the story ..... .
a) have the same senses that we **do**
b) have no sense of hearing as well as sight
c) hear the sounds of the ocean
d) live in darkness because no light reaches to the bottom
e) do not hear the sound of sea as they are accustomed to it

3. In the passage a child in darkness is likened to ....
a) someone who lives where there are no seasons
b) an animal without the sense of touch
c) a sea creature with no seeing or hearing ability
d) a deaf child unaffected by the environment
e) a perfect sleeper, for there is no sound around to hear

Passage #2
Official records state that the Pueblo Indians lived in New Mexico and Arizona. The word "Pueblo" comes from the Spanish word "pueblo," meaning town or village. The Spaniards found these Indians living in apartment houses, some of them on the side of a cliff in order that they could be reached only by ladders. Whenever they were attacked by Apaches, the Pueblos would pull up the ladders. They grew corn, which they watered with water flowing down in ditches. They wove cloth, made wonderful baskets, and created jars and pots out of clay proving how skillful they were at hand-craft.

Reading Comprehension Questions

1. From the passage we understand that the Pueblo Indians were afraid of ..... .
a) diff dwelling
b) Apache Indians
C) apartment houses
d) water flowing down in ditches
e) solitary life

2. Why the Spaniards called these Indians "Pueblos" is because they ..... .
a) were close to the Apaches
b) lived together in a town or village
c) famed and brought down water in ditches
d) pulled up their ladders when attacked
e) achieved fame thanks to their hand-craft

3. The Pueblo Indians lived on the side of a cliff ..... .
a) although they had apartment houses
b) to observe the stars in the sky for rain season
c) so that they could provide themselves **with** shelters
d) and, they didn't have a lake, a stream, or a pond
e) **as** long as they were all together

Passage #3

It was a man who lived before the time of Christopher Columbus that was the world's first great traveler. His name was Marco Polo. With his father and his uncle, he traveled from Italy to China, crossing mountains and deserts to get there. In China a king called Kublai Khan was pleased to see the Polos and had them live near to him. They stayed for twenty-three years. Kublai Khan sent Marco to other countries to do business for him. When Marco finally returned to Italy, he wrote all about his adventures in a book, which was read by Columbus and many other people, who also became interested in traveling to strange countries.

Reading Comprehension Questions

1. This story is mainly about …… .
a) **the** world's first great traveler
b) traveling from Italy to China
c) why Polo went to **the** far east
d) Marco Polo and Kublai Khan
e) in what ways Columbus affected Polo

2. The reason that Marco Polo is called great is not that …… .
a) he traveled very far to reach China for a new world
b) he wrote about his adventures in a book, which many people read
c) he was so well liked by the king of China
d) he crossed mountains and deserts to reach China
e) he achieved fame thanks to his good reasoning

3. We know from the *story* that after he turned back, ……
a) Marco brought out a book inspiring new voyages
b) Marco stayed in Italy for twenty-three years
c) Kublai Khan knew that Marco had crossed mountains and deserts
d) Kublai Khan sent Columbus to other countries for business
e) Marco set out for a new adventure

Passage #4

Have you ever wondered whether fishes drink or not? All living things must drink, and they require a fresh supply of water often. A person can go without food for many days, but he or she cannot go for long without water. Fishes drink, and fishes that live in salt water must drink salt water. However, when we watch them in an aquarium and see them opening and closing their mouths, we must not assume that they are drinking. Fishes need water for its oxygen. The water that they seem to be gulping gives them oxygen, which is in the water. On the other hand, when a fish drinks, it swallows water, just in the way we do.

Reading Comprehension Questions

1. It is stated in the passage that a fish opens and closes its mouth …… .
a) in order to **get** oxygen
c) to drink to **stay** alive
d) to swim in an aquarium.
e) so that it *can* suffice salt

2. We are informed by the passage that a person …… .
a) can live for a long time without water
b) can live for a long time without food
c) has no need for food and water
d) has no need for a fresh supply of water
e) does need water to get oxygen

Final Grammar Test

Part I: True or False

1. The following word group is a FRAGMENT: That movie, one of my favorites.
   __True
   __False

2. The following word group is a FRAGMENT: The local baseball team, needing a good pitcher most of all.
   __True
   __False

3. The following word group is a FRAGMENT: Using a flashlight, he looked under the bed for his shoes.
   __True
   __False

4. The capitalized verb agrees with the subject: Three employees from our company and one from our competitor WAS fired.
   __True
   __False

5. The capitalized verb agrees with the subject: Three of my friends LIKE this band.
   __True
   __False

6. The capitalized verb agrees with the subject: Six girls and one boy WAS in the dance class.
   __True
   __False

7. Quotation marks are correctly used in the following sentence, the entire sentence is correctly punctuated, and all words in the sentence are correctly capitalized:
   "This is a fantastic opportunity", the salesman insisted.
   __True
   __False

8. Quotation marks are correctly used in the following sentence, the entire sentence is correctly punctuated, and all words in the sentence are correctly capitalized:

"Are you serious ?!?" Fred asked.
__True
__False

9. Quotation marks are correctly used in the following sentence, the entire sentence is correctly punctuated, and all words in the sentence are correctly capitalized:
My best friend said that "She'd heard something like that."
__True
__False

Part II: Multiple Choice

In the following sentences, identify if the word grouping contains sentence fragments, a comma splice, or a run-on sentence, or if the grouping is a complete sentence.

10. Cats, unlike dogs and fond of sitting on laps.
    __ Sentence fragment
    __ Comma splice
    __ Run-on sentence
    __ Complete sentence (contains no error)

11. I don't know what you want me to do, the directions are not clear.
    __ Sentence fragment
    __ Comma splice
    __ Run-on sentence
    __ Complete sentence (contains no error)

12. While I like bacon, it is not good for me.
    __ Sentence fragment
    __ Comma splice
    __ Run-on sentence
    __ Complete sentence (contains no error)

13. I like chocolate she likes butterscotch.
    __ Sentence fragment
    __ Comma splice
    __ Run-on sentence
    __ Complete sentence (contains no error)

Identify the pronoun error in each of the following sentences.

14. When one buys insurance, you need to be clear about your needs.
    __ Pronoun shift in number
    __ Pronoun shift in person
    __ Ambiguous reference
    __ No error

15. The teacher said they were going to grade the test over the weekend.
    __ Pronoun shift in number
    __ Pronoun shift in person
    __ Ambiguous reference
    __ No error

16. Sally told Janice that she made the honor role.
    __ Pronoun shift in number
    __ Pronoun shift in person
    __ Ambiguous reference
    __ No error

17. The new employees worked long hours, hoping that doing so would advance their careers.
    __ Pronoun shift in number
    __ Pronoun shift in person
    __ Ambiguous reference
    __ No error

18. Dave hoped that Steve and __ would win the tennis tournament.
    __ him
    __ himself
    __ he
    __ his

19. Lisa hoped that Shelly had remembered to ask her mother for the chocolate chip cookies.
    __ Pronoun shift in number
    __ Pronoun shift in person
    __ Ambiguous reference
    __ No error

35

Identify the location or locations where apostrophe errors occur:

20. When we we're (A) on our way home, we were (B) eager to get they're (C).
    __Only A
    __Only B
    __Only C
    __A and C

21. Identify the location or locations where apostrophe errors occur:
    "Put the clothes over they're (A)," he said. "That is where they're (B) going."
    __Only A
    __Only B
    __A and B
    __No error

22. Identify the location or locations where apostrophe errors occur:
    When the dog knocked over it's (A) bowl, the little girl claimed that the dog wasn't (B) her's (C).
    __Only A
    __Only B
    __Only C
    __A and C

23. Which portion of this sentence followed by a letter is not parallel?
    The company president inspired his employees (A), charmed the press (B), and redefined his company's strategic plan (C).
    __A
    __B
    __C
    __No error

24. Which portion of this sentence followed by a letter is not parallel?
    The clown juggles (A), makes balloon animals (B), and will paint faces (C).
    __A
    __B
    __C
    __No error

25. Which portion of this sentence followed by a letter is not parallel?
    The retired fireman liked fishing (A), to hunt (B), and watching basketball on television (C).
    __ A
    __ B
    __ C
    __ No error

26. Choose the correct verb tenses required in the following sentence.
    Whenever I __ to the grocery, I always ___ for fresh produce.
    __ went/looked
    __ went/look
    __ go/looked
    __ had gone/look

27. Choose the appropriate irregular verb form in the following sentence.
    In light of recent developments, the company president ___ his position.
    __ rethink
    __ rethinked
    __ rethought
    __ rethoughted

28. Choose the appropriate irregular verb form in the following sentence.
    I was surprised by how successful Janice ____.
    __ become
    __ had become
    __ became
    __ had became

29. Choose the appropriate irregular verb form in the following sentence.
    In retrospect, Jason shouldn't have taken that important business call right after he'd been ___.
    __ awake
    __ awaked
    __ awakened
    __ awaken

Choose the answer that completes each sentence correctly.

30. Investing in pure research ___ yields no immediate profit, can be hard to justify when a company is in financial difficulties.
    __ who
    __ which
    __ , which
    __ that

31. I had hoped the police would blame Bruce, not ___.
    __ me
    __ myself
    __ mineself
    __ I

32. Some interviewers ____ have a clear sense of what they want in an employee, ask very tough questions.
    __ who
    __ , who
    __ which
    __ that

33. A venture capitalist has to be willing to take risks when ___ invests ___ money.
    __ they /their
    __ he / his
    __ she /her
    __ he or she /his or her

34. Many times people will ask a writer where ____ gets ____ ideas.
    __ they/their.
    __ he/his
    __ she/her
    __ he or she/his or her

Part III: Revision

In this section of the final, revise the sentences provided to correct the grammar errors indicated. (In many cases there will be more than one correct alternative to the sentence provided; credit will be given for all correct answers.)

Revise the following word groups to remove all fragments and/or parallelism errors.

35. I like baseball because it is fun and teaches me about the sport.

36. The White Sox are really good at the fundamentals of baseball. Which is why they won the World Series in 2005.

Revise the following word groups to remove all run-on sentences.

37. Studying is hard work many students find they study better when they take regular breaks.

38. Some tests are so hard that no one does well on them other tests are too easy and don't really test comprehension.

Revise the following sentences so that the subjects and verbs agree with one another.

39. One of my friends want to attend my graduation ceremony.

40. Seven cats, two monkeys, and a dog plays in the store window.

Revise the following sentences to remove all pronoun errors.

41. When a police officer fires his gun, he must fill out a lot of paperwork.

42. When a teacher writes an exam, they think about what aspects of student learning they want to test.

Revise the following sentences to remove all apostrophe errors.

43. Some people know where they parked they're car's, and some dont.

44. I gave you your's, and Im sorry if its broken now.

Revise the following sentences to make one of the existing sentences subordinate to the other.

45. The hurricane destroyed some oil rigs. Fuel prices rose.

46. People know they are going to have to retire. They often don't save enough money to do so comfortably.

MATHEMATICS REVIEW WORKBOOK

Math Prescreening Assessment

You will find a range of math tasks here. There are basic operations of addition, subtraction, multiplication and division with whole numbers, decimals and fractions. You will compute time, length, and prices, and use percentages. You will get numerical information from charts and tables and descriptive statements. This sample includes items that are about the same level of difficulty as the actual prescreening assessment. If you are comfortable with this sample, you should feel comfortable with the actual assessment.

1. Subtract   .25
                - .08

a) 17
b) 1.7
c) .17
d) .017

2. Subtract: 2007
               - 1865

a) 273
b) 173
c) 142
d) 242

3. Multiply: 3.4
              x .26

a) 88.4
b) 8.84
c) .884
d) 884

4. Divide: 6248/26

a) 24 R8
b) 240 R8
c) 241 R8
d) 24 R3

5. Add: 1/2 + 2/3 (reduce to lowest terms)

a) 1 1/6
b) 3/6
c) 3/5
d) 4/3

6. Subtract: 2/3 - 2/5 (reduce to lowest terms)

a) 1 1/15
b) 0/2
c) 6/10
d) 4/15

7. Multiply: 3/4 x 2/3 (reduce to lowest terms)

a) 1/2
b) 8/9
c) 6/7
d) 5/12

Directions: Refer to the calendar to answer the next question.

8. A patient is to return for treatment every 3 weeks. The patient's most recent treatment was September 28. When should the next treatment be scheduled?

a) September 7

b) October 5

c) October 12

d) October 19

Directions: Refer to the table to answer the next two questions.

Log of Vital Signs			
Time	Pulse	Blood Pressure	Temperature
8 PM	39		91
9 PM	40		92
10 PM	42	100/60	94
11 PM	47	110/65	97
12 AM	56	110/65	98
1 AM	58	112/65	98
2 AM	58	110/65	98

9. What time is the first record of blood pressure?

a) 8 PM

b) 10 PM

c) 1 AM

d) 2 AM

10. How many hours did it take for the temperature to rise from 92 to 98?

a) 3

b) 4

c) 5

d) 6

Directions: Refer to the clock to answer the next two questions:

11. The clinic closes at 12:00. How long until the clinic closes?

a) 2 hours 10 minutes

b) 1 hour 50 minutes

c) 1 hour 25 minutes

d) 10 hours 10 minutes

12. What time will it be in 3 hours 40 minutes?

a) 1:50

b) 5:20

c) 5:30

d) 1:55

Directions: Use the ruler to answer the next question.

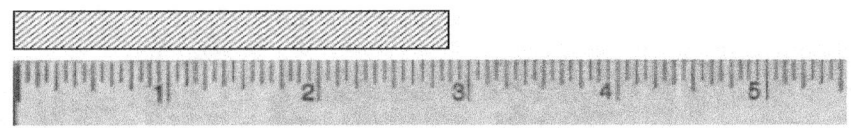

13. About how long is the shaded rectangle?

a) 2 7/8 inches

b) 5 ½ inches

c) 2 3/16 inches

d) 3 1/8 inches

Directions: Use the ruler to answer the next question.

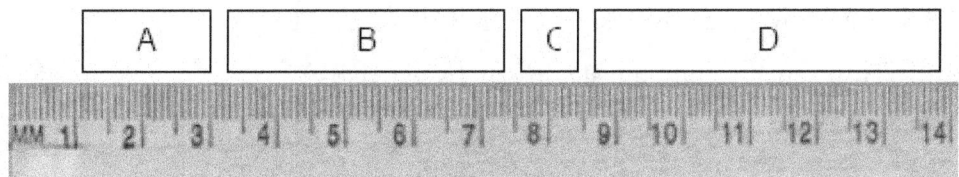

14. About how long is box A?

a) 3.0 cm

b) 1.9 cm

c) 0.3 cm

d) 1.2 cm

15. Susanna went to the farmers market with a twenty dollar bill. She spent $8.25 on strawberries. How much money does she have left?

a) $8.75
b) $11.75
c) $12.25
d) $12.75

16. You get a loan with a monthly payment of $218 for 36 months. What is the total amount you will pay?

a) $6,050
b) $6,184
c) $7,758
d) $7,848

17. A patient's chart shows that last visit she weighed 164 lbs. Today she weighs 148 lbs. How much weight did she lose between visits?

a) 24 lbs.
b) 32 lbs
c) 16 lbs.
d) 26 lbs.
A B C D

Directions: Look at the three ads for jeans to answer the next two questions.

| K. D. Nickel's 1/3 off jeans (reg. $39) | Martin's Menswear Jeans Reg. $38 HALF PRICE | Knock ¼ off the price JEANS Reg. $39 Men's Duds by Bubba |

18. How much is the current price of jeans at Men's Duds by Bubba ("1/4 off")?

a) $29.75

b) $29.25

c) $31.75

d) $10.25

19. How much do you save by buying the jeans from K. D. Nickel's?

a) $3.00

b) $13.00

c) $26.00

d) $33.00

Directions: Read the sign to answer the next question.

Hourly Truck Rental Terms

Hourly rental rate is $12, plus $0.13 per mile.

20. John rented a truck to move some furniture. He picked up the truck at 9:30AM and returned it at 1:00 PM. He drove a total of 16 miles. How much was he charged for time and mileage?

a) $67.88

b) $44.08

c) $48.00

d) $41.18

Directions: Refer to the bus schedule to answer the next two questions.

BUS SCHEDULE
OAKLAND TO FRESNO

Leave Oakland	Arrive Fresno
6:30 a.m.	11:25 a.m.
10:25 a.m.	2:35 p.m.
3:10 p.m.	7:40 p.m.
4:10 p.m.	10:05 p.m.
6:35 p.m.	10:50 p.m.
9:15 p.m.	2:25 a.m.

21. How long does the 10:25 a.m. bus take to reach Fresno?

a) 3 hours 10 minutes

b) 3 hours 50 minutes

c) 4 hours 10 minutes

d) 4 hours 50 minutes

22. Which of these busses takes the least time to get from Oakland to Fresno?

a) 6:30 a.m.

b) 10:25 a.m.

c) 3:10 p.m.

d) 6:35 p.m.

Algebra Diagnostic Pre-Test

Multiple Choice

Use the answer "NOTA" (which stands for None Of The Above) if the answer is not listed.

1. Evaluate $7m + 3mn$ when $m = 8$ and $n = 14$

A) 84

B) 196

C) 392

D) 168

E) NOTA

2. Simplify: $675 \div (6 + 9 \div 3)$

A) 15

B) 9

C) 75

D) 225

E) 135

3. $(4x^2y^3)^2 =$

A) $8x^4y^5$

B) $16x^4y^5$

C) $4x^4y^6$

D) $16x^2y^3$

E) NOTA

4. $(3x - 2)(4x + 1) =$

A) $12x^2 - 8x - 2$

B) $12x^2 + 5x - 2$

C) $x^2 - 5x - 2$

D) $12x^2 - 5x - 2$

E) NOTA

5. $(4xy^2)^{-3} =$

A) $-64x^3y^6$

B) $1/4x^3y^6$

C) $1/64x^3y^6$

D) $-4/x^3y^6$

E) NOTA

6. $(x - 4)(x + 4) =$

A) $x^2 - 16$

B) $x^2 + 16$

C) $x^2 - 8x + 16$

D) $x^2 + 8x + 16$

E) NOTA

7. Find the equation that best represents the following word problem: In a certain freshman class, the number of girls is 83 less than twice the number of boys (b). The total number of students in that freshman class is 259. How many boys and girls are in that class?

A) b + 2b = 259 - 83

B) b + 2b − 83 = 259

C) b + 83 − 2b = 259

D) b + 2b = 259

E) NOTA

8. Factor: $6x^2 - 13x - 5$

A) $(6x + 5)(x - 1)$
B) $(3x + 1)(2x - 5)$
C) $(6x - 1)(x + 5)$
D) $(2x - 1)(3x + 5)$
E) NOTA

9. Which one of the following equals a negative number?

A) $(-5) + 9$
B) $(-9) + 5$
C) $9 + 5$
D) $5 + (-9) + 4$
E) $9 - (-5)$

10. Solve the system of equations: $3x + 4y = 11$
$x - 2y = -3$

A) $x = 1$ $y = 2$
B) $x = -1$ $y = 3/4$
C) $x = 2$ $y = -3$
D) $x = 1$ $y = -2$
E) NOTA

11. Factor: $25x^2 - 16y^2$

A) $(5x - 4y)2$
B) $5(5x - 4y)$
C) $(5x + 4y)(5x - 4y)$
D) $(5x + 2y)(5x - 8y)$
E) NOTA

12. Solve: $2x^2 + 5x - 3 = 0$

A) 3, 2

B) –3, ½

C) 3/2, 1

D) 3, ½

E) NOTA

13. If $3x + y = 10$ and $x - 4y = -1$ Solve for y.

A) 1

B) 3

C) –2

D) 7/13

E) – 1

14. Solve: $1/3y + 28 = -5$

A) –11

B) 11

C) 99

D) 96

E) NOTA

15. Solve: $3x + 17 - 5x = 12 - (6x + 3)$

A) 2

B) 4

C) 0

D) – 4

E) NOTA

16. You and three friends are eating a pizza with 12 pieces. Each person eats the same number of pieces. Let x represent the number of pieces each person eats. Which of the following equations is an algebraic model for the situation?

A) $3x = 12$

B) $1/3x = 12$

C) $4x = 12$

D) $1/4x = 12$

E) NOTA

17. $(3x + 4)^2 =$

A) $9x^2 + 12x + 16$

B) $9x^2 + 16$

C) $9x^2 + 24x + 16$

D) $9x + 16$

E) $25x^2$

18. Solve: $3x(x - 4)(3x + 5) = 0$

A) 4, -5/3

B) – 4, -5/3, 3, 0

C) -5/3, 4, 0

D) 4, –5, 0

E) NOTA

19. One of the solutions of the equation: $3x^2 + 11x = 4$ is

A) 0
B) -11/3
C) 4
D) 1/3
E) NOTA

20. Simplify: $(3cd^6)^3(cd)^4$

A) $27c^7d^{10}$

B) $27c^7d^{13}$

C) $9c^7d^{22}$

D) $27c^{12}d^{72}$

E) $27c^7d^{22}$

21. Simplify: $(4c^4 + 1) - (7c^3 - 3) + (2c^4 + 5c^3)$

A) $6c^4 + 2c^3 - 4$

B) $6c^4 - 2c^3 + 4$

C) $6c^4 - 2c^3 - 2$

D) $2c^4 - 2c^3 - 2$

E) $4c + 4$

22. The number ten is raised to a power between 0 and 1. The answer has to be between which two numbers?

A) 0 and 1

B) 1 and 10

C) 10 and 100 but not 5

D) 0 and 100 but not 50

E) -10 and 0

23. Which of the following is the least?

A) .27

B) 1/4

C) 3/8

D) 2/11

E) 11%

24. If $x = 2$ and $y = -3$, then $-xy^2 =$

A) −36

B) −18

C) −12

D) 12

E) 18

25. Which is closest to the distance between A and B on the number line?

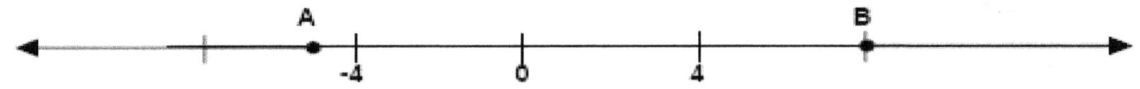

A) -9

B) -5

C) 13

D) 5

E) 12

26. Define $p \sim q$ by the equation $p \sim q = p^2q^3 - 3q$. Then $2 \sim 3 =$

A) 108

B) 27

C) 99

D) 117

E) 89

27. If $7x + 4 = -19 + 5x$, then $2x - 14$ equals

A) 23

B) -23

C) -3

D) 16

E) NOTA

28. Which of the following best describes the circled part of the statement?

$$\boxed{7x + 9} = 40$$

A) Coefficient

B) Variable

C) Term

D) Expression

E) Solution

29. Solve for x:

$5x - 10 = 2 - 2x + 10(x - 3)$

A) 6

B) 3

C) -3

D) -14

E) NOTA

Percent and Ratio Practice Questions

1. Express fourteen hundredths as a percent.
    A. 0.14%
    B. 14%
    C. 0.014%
    D. 1.4%

2. 3 is what percent of 50?
    A. 3%
    B. 4%
    C. 5%
    D. 6%

3. The ratio of 2:10 is the same as what percentage?
    A. 2%
    B. 5%
    C. 10%
    D. 20%

4. Lauren had $80 in her savings account. When she received her paycheck, she made a deposit which brought the balance up to $120. By what percentage did the total amount in her account increase as a result of this deposit?
    A. 50%
    B. 40%
    C. 35%
    D. 80%

5. Round to the nearest whole number: What is 17/68, as a percent?

   A. 17%

   B. 25%

   C. 40%

   D. 68%

6. Round to the nearest whole number: Gerald made 13 out of the 22 shots he took in the basketball game. What was his shooting percentage?

   A. 13%

   B. 22%

   C. 59%

   D. 67%

7. Change the following fraction to the simplest possible ratio: 8/14

   A. 4:3

   B. 4:6

   C. 4:7

   D. 3:4

8. If 5 people buy 3 pens each and 3 people buy 7 pencils each, what is the ratio of the total number of pens to the total number of pencils?

   A. 15:21

   B. 3:7

   C. 5:3

   D. 1:1

9. In a town, the ratio of men to women is 2:1. If the number of women in the town is doubled, what will be the new ratio of men to women?

   A. 1:2

   B. 1:1

   C. 2:1

   D. 3:1

10. A man's lawn grass is 3 inches high. He mows the lawn and cuts off 30% of its height. How tall will the grass be after the lawn is mowed?

    A. 0.9 inches

    B. 2.1 inches

    C. 2.7 inches

    D. 2.9 inches

NOTES

Percentage Word Problems Worksheet 1

1. Stuart made fruit juice using oranges and grapes. Sixty percent of fruits are oranges. If he used a total of 60 oranges, how many grapes should he use?

2. Dick just hired a new employee to work in your bakeshop. In one hour the employee burned 55 chocolate chip cookie. If this represented 15% of the day's production, how many cookies did you plan on producing that day?

3. The monthly budget for the front house is $18,000. You spent 9% of the budget on fresh flowers. How many did you spend on fresh flowers?

4. Your food costs are $5,500. Your total food sales are $11,000. What percent of your food sales do the food costs represent?

5. You have a large container of olive oil. You have used 25 quarts of oil. Twenty-five percent of the olive oil remain. How many quarts of olive oil remain?

6. A serving of ice cream contains 4200 calories. 1260 calories come from fat. What percent of the total calories come from fat?

7. The chef has 50 pounds of strip loin. The trim loss on the strip loin is 60% and the cooked loss is 20% of the trimmed weight. How many pounds of trimmed, cooked strip loin will the chef have left to serve to his customers?

8. Calculate 4.5% of 600kg.

9. Calculate 25% of 700cm.

10. Out of 3500 students of a school, only 36% passed. Find how many students failed.

Percentage Word Problems Worksheet 2

1. Janelle made a fruit cake using bananas and apples. Forty percent of fruits are bananas. If she used a total of 120 fruits, how many apples should she use?

2. John just hired a new employee to work in your bakeshop. In one hour the employee burned 150 chocolate chip cookies. If this represented 15% of the day's production, how many chocolate chip cookies did you plan on producing that day?

3. The monthly budget for the front house is $51,000. You spent 17% of the budget on fresh flowers. How many did you spend on fresh flowers?

4. Your food costs are $2,250. Your total food sales are $25,000. What percent of your food sales do the food costs represent?

5. You have a large container of olive oil. You have used 25 quarts of oil. Twenty-five percent of the olive oil remain. How many quarts of olive oil remain?

6. A serving of ice cream contains 6400 calories. 1600 calories come from fat. What percent of the total calories come from fat?

7. The chef has 80 pounds of strip loin. The trim loss on the strip loin is 55% and the cooked loss is 60% of the trimmed weight. How many pounds of trimmed, cooked strip loin will the chef have left to serve to his customers?

8. Calculate 55% of 900kg?

9. Calculate 86% of 500cm?

10. Out of 6700 students of a school, only 90% passed. Find how many students failed.

Mean, Median and Mode

Measures of central tendency, or averages, are used in a variety of contexts and form the basis of statistics.

Mean (Arithmetic Mean)

To calculate the arithmetic mean of a set of data, we must first add up (sum) all of the data values (x) and then divide the result by the number of values (n).

Example

Find the mean of: 6, 8, 11, 5, 2, 9, 7, 8

$6 + 8 + 11 + 5 + 2 + 9 + 7 + 8 = 56$ $56/8 = 7$

Median

The median value of a set of data is the middle value of the ordered data. That is, the data must be put in numerical order first.

Find the median of the following:

a) 11, 4, 9, 7, 10, 5, 6

Ordering the data gives 4, 5, 6, 7, 9, 10, 11 and the middle value is 7.

b) 1, 3, 0.5, 0.6, 2, 2.5, 3.1, 2.9

Ordering the data gives 0.5, 0.6, 1, 2, 2.5 2.9, 3, 3.1

Here there is a middle pair 2 and 2.5. The median is between these 2 values i.e. the mean of them $(2+2.5)/2 = 2.25$

Mode

The modal value of a set of data is the most frequently occurring value.

Find the mode for:

2, 6, 3, 9, 5, 6, 2, 6

It can be seen that the most frequently occurring value is 6. (There are 3 of these).

Exercises

1. Find the mode, median and mean of the following:
a) 3, 12, 11, 7, 5, 5, 6, 4, 10
b) 16, 19, 10, 24, 19
c) 8, 2, 8, 5, 5, 8
d) 28, 39, 42, 29, 39, 40, 36, 46, 41, 30
e) 133, 215, 250, 108, 206, 159, 206, 178
f) 76, 94, 76, 82, 78, 86, 90
g) 52, 61, 49, 52, 49, 52, 41, 58

2. The exchange route for sterling against the US dollar for 15 days in January 2003 is given in the following table. Calculate the mean, median and mode of this data.

1.5977 1.6028 1.6108 1.6067 1.5995 1.6064 1.6080 1.6054
1.6098 1.6049 1.6064 1.6179 1.6082 1.6095 1.6134

3. The following data is the hourly pay in pounds offered to shop assistants in a survey of job vacancies for June 2003 based in Reading. Calculate the mean, median, and mode of this data.

5.00 4.21 4.97 5.00 5.00 5.29 5.05 5.50 5.79 5.00 5.40
5.20 5.10 5.06 4.50 4.50 5.50 4.50 5.00 5.00 5.50

Distance, Rate, and Time

The formula Distance = Rate x Time expresses one of the most frequently used relations in algebra.

Since an equation remains true as long as you divide through by the same non-zero element on each side, this formula can be written in different ways:
   To find **rate**, divide through on both sides by *time:*

$$\text{Rate} = \frac{\text{Distance}}{\text{Time}}$$

Rate is distance (given in units such as miles, feet, kilometers, meters, etc.) divided by time (hours, minutes, seconds, etc.). Rate can always be written as a fraction that has distance units in the numerator and time units in the denominator, e.g., 25 miles/1 hour.
   To find **time**, divide through on both sides by *rate:*

$$\text{Time} = \frac{\text{Distance}}{\text{Rate}}$$

When using this equation, it's important to keep the units straight. For instance, if the rate the problem gives is in miles per hour (mph), then the time needs to be in hours, and the distance in miles. If the time is given in minutes, you will need to divide by 60 to convert it to hours before you can use the equation to find the distance in miles. Always make your units match: if the time is given in fortnights and the distance in furlongs, then the rate should be given in furlongs per fortnight.

You can see why this is true if you look carefully at how the units are expressed. Say a car is travelling at 30 mph and you want to figure out how far it will go in 2 hours. You can use the formula:

   Rate x Time = Distance

Practice using the formula.

1) An aircraft carrier made a trip to Guam and back. The trip there took three hours and the trip back took four hours. It averaged 6km/h on the return trip. Find the average speed of the trip there.

2) A passenger plane made a trip to Las Vegas and back. On the trip there it flew 432 mph and on the return trip it went 480 mph. How long did the trip there take if the return trip took nine hours?

3) A cattle train left Miami and traveled toward New York. 14 hours later a diesel train left traveling at 45 km/h in an effort to catch up to the cattle train. After traveling for four hours the diesel train finally caught up. What was the cattle train's average speed?

4) Jose left the White House and drove toward the recycling plant at an average speed of 40 km/h. Rob left some time later driving in the same direction at an average speed of 48km/h. After driving for five hours Rob caught up with Jose. How long did Jose drive before Rob caught up?

5) A cargo plane flew to the maintenance facility and back. It took one hour less time to get there than it did to get back. The average speed on the trip there was 220 mph. The average speed on the way back was 200 mph. How many hours did the trip there take?

6) Kali left school and traveled toward her friend's house at an average speed of 40 km/h. Matt left one hour later and traveled in the opposite direction with an average speed of 50 km/h. Find the number of hours Matt needs to travel before they are 400 km apart.

7) Ryan left the science museum and drove south. Gabriella left three hours later driving 42 km/h faster in an effort to catch up to him. After two hours Gabriella finally caught up. Find Ryan's average speed.

8) A submarine left Hawaii two hours before an aircraft carrier. The vessels traveled in opposite directions. The aircraft carrier traveled at 25 mph for nine hours. After this time the vessels were 280 mi. apart. Find the submarine's speed.

9) Chelsea left the White House and traveled toward the capital at an average speed of 34km/h. Jasmine left at the same time and traveled in the opposite direction with an average speed of 65 km/h. Find the number of hours Jasmine needs to travel before they are 59.4 km apart.

10) Jose left the airport and traveled toward the mountains. Kayla left 2.1 hours later traveling 35 mph faster in an effort to catch up to him. After 1.2 hours Kayla finally caught up. Find Jose's average speed.

Mathematics Review Guide

Part I: Arithmetic Review

Arithmetic covers the following topics: operations with whole numbers, fractions, decimals, ratios and proportions, and percents.

Directions: All fractions and ratios must be reduced completely. Write your answers on the answer sheet.

Operations with Fractions

1. Reduce the fraction to lowest terms: 28/42

a. 14/21

b. 4/6

c. 2/3

d. 7/10

2. Find the product: 7/16 × 24/35

a. 3/10

b. 31/51

c. 595/384

d. 384/595

3. Divide: 4/7 ÷ 3/4

a. 3/7

b. 16/21

c. 7/3

d. 21/16

4. Multiply: (3 ¼)(6 ⅔)

a. 18 ⅙

b. 13 ¾

c. 18 ¼

d. 21 ⅔

Operations with Decimals

5. Add: 4.23 + 3.7 + 2.006

a. 24.66

b. 9.36

c. 9.936

d. 9.306

6. Write 17/10 as a decimal number.

a. .17

b. 1.7

c. 17

7. Round 1928.956 to the tenths place.

a. 1928.9

b. 1929.0

c. 1928.95

d. 1928.96

8. If one square yard of carpet costs $15.45, how much will 45.5 square yards cost?

a. $702.98

b. $2.95

c. $7,029.75

d. $70.30

9. If Angie's gross pay for 21.5 hours was $141.04, what was her pay per hour?

a. $15.24/hr

b. $6.72/hr

c. $6.56/hr

d. $7.29/hr

Operations with Ratios and Proportions

10. Two inches on a map equals 10 miles. Write the ratio of map inches to miles.

a. 1:5

b. 5:1

c. 2:0

d. 2:1

11. Find the missing part of the proportion: 12/x = 3/7

a. 36

b. 24

c. 21

d. 28

12. If it takes Tom 48 minutes to walk 3 miles, how many minutes will it take him to walk 5 miles?

a. 16 min.

b. 144 min.

c. 15 min.

d. 80 min.

Operations with Percentages

13. Change the percent to a fraction: 145%

a. 29/20

b. 29/2

c. 9/50

d. 29/5

14. Change the decimal number to a percent: .129

a. 1.29%

b. 12.9%

c. 129%

d. .129%

15. Frost's Refrigeration decided to increase their basic service call charge by 8%. What will be the new charge for a service call if they had been charging $42.50?

a. $44.80

b. $45.00

c. $45.20

d. $45.90

Part II: Introduction to Elementary Algebra Review Guide

Introduction to Elementary Algebra covers the following topics: introduction to variables, operations with signed numbers, solutions to linear equations and inequalities, operations with positive integer exponents, evaluation and manipulations of formulas, and solving basic word problems.

Operations with Signed Numbers

16. Simplify: (5 − 2) − (2 − 5)

a. 3

b. 0

c. 6

d. −6

17. Simplify: $\dfrac{9+21}{3} - \dfrac{12(4)}{2}$

a. −14

b. −16

c. -18/5

d. −1

Variables

18. Translate to an algebraic expression: Twice the sum of 3x and y

a. 2(3x) + y

b. 6x + 2y

c. 3x + 2y

d. 2 + 3x + y

19. Evaluate: (x – 3y) (2x + y) when x = -2 and y = -1

a. 25

b. –25

c. –3

d. –5

20. Simplify: 6x – 7b – 10x + 11b

a. –x + b

b. –4x + 4b

c. 4x – 4b

d. –4x – 4b

21. Simplify: 3(x + 1) – 4(x – 1)

a. –x – 7

b. –x – 1

c. –x + 7

d. –x + 1

22. Multiply: (4a/9b) (-3b/16a)

a. ab/12ab

b. 1/12

c. -12

d. -1/12

23. Simplify: 2[9 x – 2(3 x – 2)]

a. 6x – 2

b. 6x – 4

c. 6x + 4

d. 6x + 8

Solutions to Linear Equations and Inequalities

24. Solve: -2x + 21 = -11

a. –5

b. –16

c. 16

d. 5

25. Solve: 2x/3 = 4/5

a. 6/5

b. 8/15

c. 12/5

d. 20/15

26. Solve: 2x + 6 > 3x + 32

a. x > -26

b. x > -38

c. x < -26

d. x < 26

27. Solve: 6(x − 5) − 3x = -9

a. −13

b. 7

c. 13

d. −7

Operations with Positive Integer Exponents

28. Simplify: $2^2 − (-2)^3$

a. −2

b. 12

c. 10

d. 14

29. Simplify: $(2 + 3)^2 − (2 + 3^2)$

a. 14

b. 0

c. 2

d. 32

Solving Basic Word Problems

30. A board is 28 feet long and is cut into three pieces. The second piece is twice as long as the first piece and the third is three feet longer than the second. What is the length of each piece?

a. 5, 10, 13

b. 4, 8, 16

c. 6, 12, 10

d. 8, 16, 4

31. The perimeter of a rectangle is 66 feet and the width is 7 feet. What is the length in feet?

a. 26

b. 52

c. 40

d. 20

32. The area of a triangle is 24 square feet. If the base is 12 feet, what is the height of the triangle?

a. 4

b. 2

c. 8

d. 6

33. Seven less than four times a number is 35. What is the number?

a. 7

b. 21/2

c. –7

d. -21/2

Manipulation of Formulas

34. Solve: $v = k + gt$ for t

a. $t = (v + g)/ k$

b. $t = (v - g)/ k$

c. $t = (v + k)/g$

d. $t = (v - k)/g$

Part III: Elementary Algebra

Polynomials

35. Subtract $(2x + 1)$ from the sum of $(3x - 7)$ and $(5x + 2)$

a. $6x - 6$

b. $-6x + 6$

c. $4x + 10$

d. $4x - 10$

36. Multiply: $(x + 3)(5x - 1)$

a. $5x^2 + 14x - 3$

b. $5x^2 + 15x - 3$

c. $5x^2 - x - 3$

d. $5x^2 + 16x - 3$

DATA INTERPRETATION

& REASONING WORKBOOK

Analytical Reasoning Test

The focus of the practice exercise is on the Analytical Reasoning section, but it also deals with the Logical Reasoning Section to the extent that understanding and responding to those questions depends on language skills.

Question 1-3

Three men (Tom, Peter and Jack) and three women (Eliza, Anne and Karen) are spending a few months at a hillside. They are to stay in a row of nine cottages, each one living in his or her own cottage. There are no others staying in the same row of houses.

1. Anne, Tom and Jack do not want to stay in any cottage, which is at the end of the row.
2. Eliza and Anne are unwilling to stay besides any occupied cottage.
3. Karen is next to Peter and Jack.
4. Between Anne and Jack's cottage there is just one vacant house.
5. None of the girls occupy adjacent cottages.
6. The house occupied by Tom is next to an end cottage.

1. Which of the above statements can be said to have been derived from two other statements?
(a) Statement 1
(b) Statement 2
(c) Statement 3
(d) Statement 5
(e) Statement 6

2. How many of them occupy cottages next to a vacant cottage?
(a) 2
(b) 3
(c) 4
(d) 5
(e) 6

3. Which among these statement(s) are true?
I. Anne is between Eliza and Jack.
II. At the most four persons can have occupied cottages on either side of them.
III. Tom stays besides Peter
(a) I only
(b) II only

(c) I and III only
(d) II and III only
(e) I, II and III

Questions 4-5

An employee has been assigned the task of allotting offices to six of the staff members. The offices are numbered 1 - 6. The offices are arranged in a row and they are separated from each other by six foot high dividers. Hence voices, sounds and cigarette smoke flow easily from one office to another.

Miss Robert's needs to use the telephone quite often throughout the day. Mr. Mike and Mr. Brown need adjacent offices as they need to consult each other often while working. Miss. Hardy, is a senior employee and has to be allotted the office number 5, having the biggest window.

Mr. Donald requires silence in the offices next to his. Mr. Tim, Mr. Mike and Mr. Donald are all smokers. Miss Hardy finds tobacco smoke allergic and consecutively the offices next to hers to be occupied by non-smokers.

Unless specifically stated all the employees maintain an atmosphere of silence during office hours.

4. The ideal candidate to occupy the office furthest from Mr. Brown would be
(a) Miss Hardy
(b) Mr. Mike
(c) Mr. Tim
(d) Mr. Donald
(e) Mr. Robert

5. The three employees who are smokers should be seated in which offices?

(a) 1, 2 and 4
(b) 2, 3 and 6
(c) 1, 2 and 3
(d) 1, 3 and 5
(e) 1, 2 and 6

85

Data Interpretation Practice Exercises

States over the Years

State	Year									
	1997		1998		1999		2000		2001	
	App.	Qual.	App.	Qual.	App.	Qual.	App.	Qual.	App.	Qual.
M	5200	720	8500	980	7400	850	6800	775	9500	1125
N	7500	840	9200	1050	8450	920	9200	980	8800	1020
P	6400	780	8800	1020	7800	890	8750	1010	9750	1250
Q	8100	950	9500	1240	8700	980	9700	1200	8950	995
R	7800	870	7600	940	9800	1350	7600	945	7990	885

1. Total number of candidates qualified from all the states together in 1997 is approximately what percentage of the total number of candidates qualified from all the states together in 1998?

A. 72%
B. 77%
C. 80%
D. 83%

2. What is the average candidates who appeared from State Q during the given years?

A. 8700
B. 8760
C. 8990
D. 8920

3. The percentage of total number of qualified candidates to the total number of appeared candidates among all the five states in 1999 is?

A. 11.49%
B. 11.84%
C. 12.21%
D. 12.57%

4. Combining the states P and Q together in 1998, what is the percentage of the candidates qualified to that of the candidate appeared?

A. 10.87%
B. 11.49%
C. 12.35%
D. 12.54%

Study the following pie chart and answer the questions based on them.

The following pie-chart shows the percentage distribution of the expenditure incurred in publishing a book. Study the pie-chart; then answer the questions based on it.

Various Expenditures (in percentage) Incurred in Publishing a Book

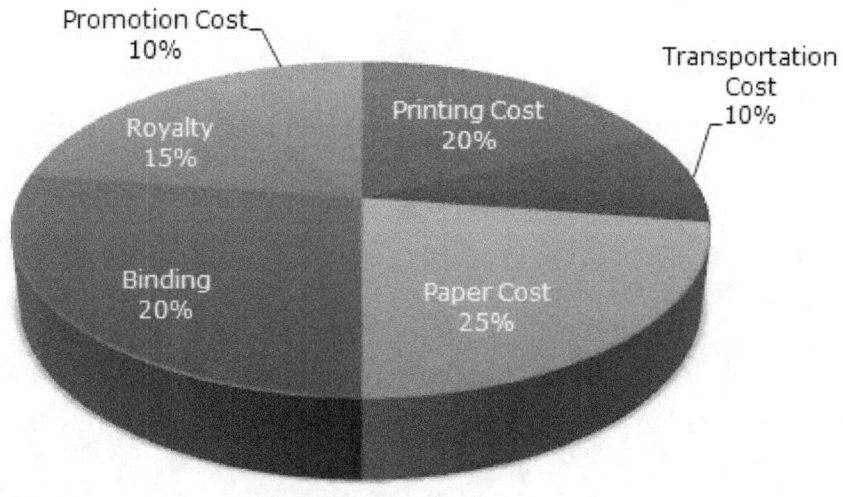

5. If for a certain quantity of books, the publisher has to pay Rs. 30,600 as printing cost, then what will be amount of royalty to be paid for these books?
   A. Rs. 19,450
   B. Rs. 21,200
   C. Rs. 22,950
   D. Rs. 26,150

6. What is the central angle of the sector corresponding to the expenditure incurred on Royalty?
   A. 15°
   B. 24°
   C. 54°
   D. 48°

Study the following bar graph and answer the questions based on it.

The bar graph given below shows the sales of books (in thousand number) from six branches of a publishing company during two consecutive years 2000 and 2001.

Sales of Books (in thousand numbers) from Six Branches - B1, B2, B3, B4, B5 and B6 of a publishing Company in 2000 and 2001.

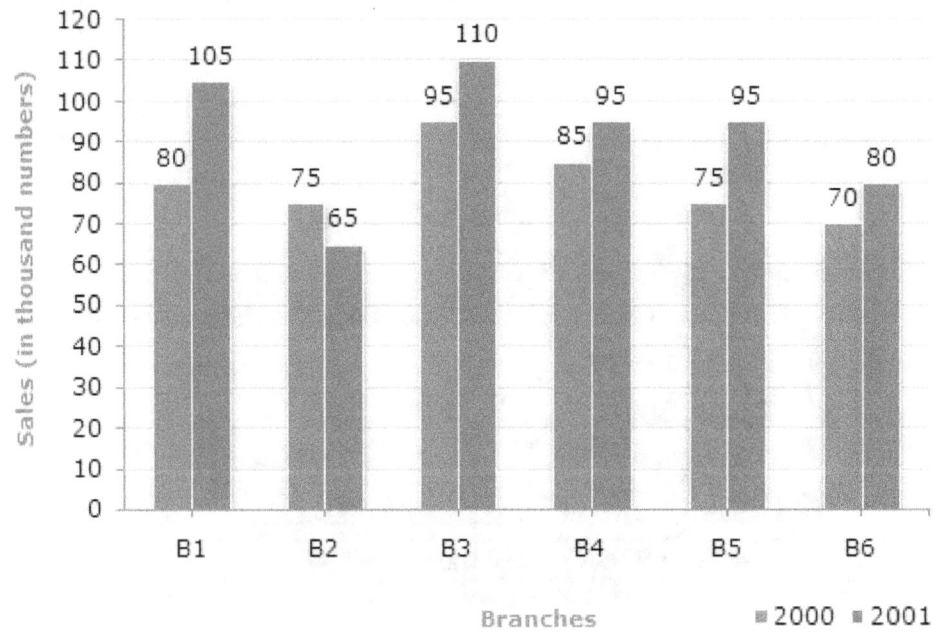

7. What is the ratio of the total sales of branch B2 for both years to the total sales of branch B4 for both years?
   A. 2:3
   B. 3:5
   C. 4:5
   D. 7:9

8. Total sales of branch B6 for both the years is what percent of the total sales of branches B3 for both the years?
A. 68.54%
B. 71.11%
C. 73.17%
D. 75.55%

Numerical Reasoning Practice

Question 1
Find the missing number in the following series:

234567	23456	?	234	23
A: 6	B: 2356	C: 2347	D: 2345	E: None of these

Question 2
The numbers in the grid go together in a certain way.
Which number should be in the square marked by the question mark?

14	16	18
16	18	20
18	20	?

A: 21   B: 22   C: 24   D: 26   E: None of these

Question 3
One container has 28 kilograms of flour and another has 4 kilograms.
How many kilograms must be taken from one container, so each has an equal amount of flour?

A: 4   B: 12   C: 16   D: 24   E: None of these

Question 4
The numbers and letters in the grid form a pattern and one of the lines has been erased.
Which number or letter should be in the square marked by the question mark?

2	A	4	A	6	A
C	B	4	B	6	B
4	4	4	C	6	C
		?			
6	6	6	6	6	E
K	J	I	H	G	F

A: D   B: F   C: 5   D: E   E: None of these

Question 5
Six pairs of shoes cost as much as 1 coat, 2 pairs of jeans cost as much as 3 pairs of shoes, and 4 pairs of socks cost as much as one pair of jeans. How many coats could I exchange for 64 pairs of socks?

A: 4   B: 1   C: 2   D: 3   E: None of these

Question 6
The numbers in the circles go together in a certain way.
Find the missing number marked by the question mark:

(169, 13)   (49, 7)   (144, ?)   (81, 9)

A: 12   B: 13   C: 11   D: 15   E: None of these

Question 7
The clock in my lounge room is 10 minutes slower than the clock on my phone, which is 6 minutes slow. My tram always leaves 6 minutes early, although it is scheduled for 8:55am. It takes me 20 minutes to get to the tram stop.
What time must I leave, according to my lounge room clock, in order to catch my tram?

    A: 8:49am   B: 8.35am   C: 8.23am   D: 8.29am   E: None of these

Question 8
A container of soft drink was shared between four work teams of employees. The first team took 1/3 of the soft drink, the second team took ½ of what was left, and the remaining two teams shared the remaining soft drink equally between them. If there were originally 240 litres of soft drink, how many litres of soft drink did the third team get?

    A: 20   B: 40   C: 80   D: 160   E: None of these

Question 9
Working mothers who earn $30,000 or less per year receive a rebate on before and after school care of 75%, plus a school bonus of $6,000 that only applies to this category of earnings. Each dollar earned above this amount and up to $40,000 reduces the rebate to 55%, and for any amount above this, the rebate drops to 30%. There are three mothers – Jade earns $40,001, Emily earns $38,000 and Lucy earns $29,550. If the cost of before and after school care is $10,000 per year, what amount of money does the person have who has the least amount of money left after paying for before and after school care?

    A: $33,000   B: $30,000   C: $40,001   D: $40,000   E: None of these

Question 10
Find the missing number in the following series:
    4   8   ?   32   64   128

    A: 24   B: 19   C: 16   D: 8   E: None of these

Question 11
Find the missing number in the following series:
    ?   85   81   83   79   81   77

    A: 89   B: 83   C: 87   D: 80   E: None of these

Question 12
The numbers in the grid go together in a certain way.
Which number should be in the square marked by the question mark?

35	30	27
31	26	23
28	23	?

    A: 19   B: 20   C: 21   D: 18   E: None of these

Question 13
Percy rides his scooter to the station, which is 10 kilometres away. If Percy rides at a steady pace of 20 kilometres per hour, how many minutes will it take him to ride from home to the station?

    A: 2   B: 4   C: 40   D: 30   E: None of these

Question 14
If Bert had 3 cents more he would have twice as much as Georgia. If he had 4 cents less, he would have the same amount.
How many cents does Bert have?
A: 4   B: 7   C: 11   D: 14   E: None of these

The following story relates to the next two questions.
Arthur, Ronald and Dianne each have a pile of socks. Mr Sockman's sock collection is worth half the value of Ronald's sock collection plus one white sock, one grey sock and one black sock.

3 X black socks	8 X black socks	4 X black socks
2 X white socks	1 X white socks	1 X white socks
1 X grey sock		3 X grey socks

Arthur's Socks   **Ronald's Socks**   **Dianne's Socks**

Black socks fetch one quarter of the price of white ones at auction, whilst greys fetch half.

Question 15
Who has the least variety of socks in their collection?
A: Ronald   B: Arthur   C: Dianne   D: Mr Sockman   E: None of these

Question 16
Who would get the most money for their sock collection at auction?
A: Ronald   B: Arthur   C: Dianne   D: Mr Sockman   E: None of these

---

Question 17
The numbers in the circles go together in a certain way.
Find the missing number marked by the question mark:

(180, 14)   (120, 8)   (?, 4)   (220, 18)

A: 70   B: 80   C: 60   D: 40   E: None of these

Question 18
The numbers in the grid go together in a certain way. One of the squares has a * placed in it, to hide the number underneath.
Which number should be in the square marked by the question mark?

32	26	22
27	?	17
22	16	*

A: 21   B: 14   C: 20   D: 10   E: None of these

Question 19
There are 72 apples on my tree at home; 38 are red, and the rest are green. I know 46 of the apples have worms in them, so I can't use them for cooking.

What is the maximum number of green apples I could have left to cook with?

A: 0	B: 8	C: 12	D: 26	E: None of these

Question 20
Rebecca must give 5 out of every 6 dollars she earns each week to the tax department. If Rebecca gets to keep $10 this week, how much did she earn in total this week?
A: $30	B: $56	C: $50	D: $60	E: None of these

Question 21
Find the missing number in the following series:

64   16   32   8   ?

A: 2	B: 8	C: 16	D: 32	E: None of these

Question 22
If a piece of blueberry pie costs $4 and a piece of apple pie costs 50% more than a piece of blueberry pie, how much does a piece of apple pie cost?
A: $3	B: $2	C: $5	D: $6	E: None of these

Question 23
Find the missing number in the following series:

4   ?   17   51   56   168

A: 8	B: 10	C: 12	D: 14	E: None of these

Question 24
Oliver has a box of toy cars, but he is not sure how many he has. If he arranges the cars in groups of four, he has three left over. If he arranges them in groups of 3, he has two left over and there are three left over when he puts them in groups of five. Oliver definitely doesn't have any more than 30 cars, so how many does he have?
A: 27	B: 28	C: 21	D: 22	E: None of these.

Question 25
From home, Mary's work is two thirds along the way to training. Training is 2.5km from work. Mary normally goes to work, then training and then home again. However, today she forgot her shoes. How far will Mary travel in total today if she has to go home before training to get her shoes?

A: 28km	B: 15km	C: 20km	D: 25km	E: None of these

Question 26
A sequence of numbers is changing by the same amount each time. The third, fourth and fifth numbers are 6, 2, and -2. What is the sum of the first eight items in the sequence?
A: -64	B: 0	C: 70	D: 14	E: None of these

Question 27
Find the missing number in the following series:

?   14   98   686   4802

A: 3	B: 4	C: 7	D: 9	E: None of these

Question 28
The numbers in each box go together in a certain way.
Find the missing number marked by the question mark:

5, 10, 25	9, 18, 81	4, 8, 16	8, 16, ?

A: 24	B: 32	C: 64	D: 128	E: None of these

Question 29
It takes 1.5 litres of sugar soap to wash a square metre of ceiling and 0.5 litres of sugar soap to wash a square metre of wall. Bianca's room is 4 metres high and each wall is 5 metres wide. There is one window, which is 4m^2 and a door, which is 9m^2.
How much sugar soap will Bianca need, assuming she does not wash the door or window (a room has four walls and a roof)?

A: 33.5 litres   B: 67 litres   C: 71 litres   D: 77.5 litres   E: None of these

Question 30
Two numbers are each multiplied by themselves to give two new numbers. The difference between these two new numbers is less than ten; the difference between the two original numbers was one. *The two original numbers added together was more than 7. What is one of the original numbers?*

A: 1   B: 2   C: 3   D: 4   E: None of these

Question 31
The novels on Suzanne's bookshelf have a combined total of 672 pages. If each novel has 4 chapters and there are 6 pages per chapter, how many novels are there altogether?

A: 26   B: 24   C: 28   D: 27   E: None of these

Question 32
Mandy finds she can get a discount on corn cobs if she buys in bulk. She can get 100 kilograms of corn cobs for $160 from Matt, on condition that she buys at least 100 kilograms. From another supplier, Robert, she can buy small quantities of corn cobs (100 or less) for $1 per cob or larger quantities (more than 100) for $0.60 per cob. Mandy charges all of her customers by weight, so she gets $5 per kilogram of corn cobs or $1.25 for an individual corn cob. If Mandy is going to sell over 100 kilograms of corn cobs today, what is the best profit per corn cob she can make?

A: $0.65   B: $0.85   C: $0.80   D: $0.60   E: None of these.

The following story relates to the next three questions.

Ms Smith	Ms Able
1 X t-shirts	1 X t-shirts
2 X pants	1 X pants
4 X jumpers	3 X jumpers

T-shirts = $7   Pants= $4   Jumpers= $3.50

Ms Smith and Ms Able are selling used clothes at a trash and treasure stall. The prices are shown above.
Ms Able calculates that half of the money she took is profit. Ms Smith is the same, except for her jumpers- she makes $1 of profit per jumper. <u>Takings</u> (the prices listed above) are the money they take from customers overall. <u>Profit</u> is what they have left over after they have paid all of their expenses.

Question 33
If both sell all of their used clothes, how much money will the person who takes the most get?

A: $28.50   B: $29   C: $31.50   D: $35   E: None of these

Question 34
How much profit will Ms Able make?

A: $29   B: $28.50   C: $14.50   D: $11.50   E: None of these

www.ingramcontent.com/pod-product-compliance
Lightning Source LLC
Chambersburg PA
CBHW081828230426
43668CB00017B/2408